Home Office Research Study 207

The 'road to nowhere':
the evidence for travelling criminals

Paul Wiles
Andrew Costello

Research, Development and Statistics Directorate
Home Office

Home Office Research Studies

The Home Office Research Studies are reports on research undertaken by or on behalf of the Home Office. They cover the range of subjects for which the Home Secretary has responsibility. Titles in the series are listed at the back of this report (copies are available from the address on the back cover). Other publications produced by the Research, Development and Statistics Directorate include Research Findings, the Research Bulletin, Statistical Bulletins and Statistical Papers.

The Research, Development and Statistics Directorate (RDS)

RDS is part of the Home Office. The Home Office's purpose is to build a safe, just and tolerant society in which the rights and responsibilities of individuals, families and communities are properly balanced and the protection and security of the public are maintained.

RDS is also a part of the Government Statistical Service (GSS). One of the GSS aims is to inform Parliament and the citizen about the state of the nation and provide a window on the work and performance of government, allowing the impact of government policies and actions to be assessed.

Therefore -

Research, Development and Statistics Directorate exists to improve policy making, decision taking and practice in support of the Home Office purpose and aims, to provide the public and Parliament with information necessary for informed debate and to publish information for future use.

"The views expressed in this report are those of the authors, not necessarily those of the Home Office (nor do they reflect Government policy)."

First published 2000

Application for reproduction should be made to the Communications and Development Unit, Room 201, Home Office, 50 Queen Anne's Gate, London SW1H 9AT.

© Crown copyright 2000   ISBN 1 84082 529 4
ISSN 0072 6435

Foreword

It is commonly assumed that greater mobility in contemporary society has led to offenders travelling longer distances to commit crime, particularly in affluent rural areas. This report examines offender's travel-to-crime patterns using a geographical information system to explore offender and victim mobility in relation to burglary and car crime. The most important finding from the research is that most offenders tend to commit crime in areas local to where they live or spend their leisure time. The evidence for this came from police recorded crime data, confirmed by data collected in interviews with convicted offenders and an analysis of the Forensic Science Service DNA database. The fact that this finding was evident in the recorded crime data highlights the value of analysing readily available data that is routinely collected by the police. This can be used for crime pattern analysis purposes and for the strategic management of high volume crime.

Carole F Willis
Head of the Policing and Reducing Crime Unit
Research, Development and Statistics Directorate
Home Office
September 2000

Acknowledgements

Thanks are due to a great number of people. In particular we would like to mention Chief Superintendent Mick Burdis (Head of C.I.D. at South Yorkshire Police), Inspector Gary Day, and Sergeant Andy Harries and Helene Mason (all of North Yorkshire Police), Lesley Boucher (the Forensic Science Service), Tony Watson (of P.I.T.O.) and especially Mike Glover who expertly conducted the offender interviews.

Thanks are due to Tim Read, Gloria Laycock and Barry Webb, of the Policing and Reducing Crime Unit, of the Research, Development and Statistics Directorate of the Home Office, for their encouragement, support and patience.

The authors

Paul Wiles at the time this research was carried out was Professor of Criminology at the University of Sheffield. He is now Director of the Research, Development and Statistics Directorate of the Home Office.

Andrew Costello is South Yorkshire Police Authority Research Fellow in the Centre for Criminological Studies, Faculty of Law, University of Sheffield.

Contents

Summary

It is often assumed that because travel has become much easier in the contemporary period then offenders must be taking advantage of this fact and travelling further to commit their crimes. There is a widely held view within police forces that a considerable amount of high volume crime is committed by travelling, often urban offenders taking advantage of increasingly easy mobility.

The present report examines these beliefs and attempts to identify the extent to which there is evidence to support them. It is based on research using geocoded police recorded crime statistics and DNA records to analyse offender travel patterns. In addition, the researchers interviewed a sample of offenders about their travels to crime. The research mainly focuses on volume crime which for this purpose was defined as burglary and TWOC.

The main findings are:

- the vast majority of offender movements are relatively short;

- much travel associated with crime is not primarily driven by plans to offend but appears to be much more dependent upon opportunities presenting themselves during normal routines;

- when offenders do travel to offend it is overwhelmingly local in nature; and

- even when longer-range travel is involved in offending elsewhere this is mainly in places which have strong traditional connections with the offender's home location.

- there was little evidence that offender's travelling to offend was significantly increasing compared with the past or that new travel opportunities were changing traditional travel patterns used by offenders.

Whilst these findings were confirmed by interview data with offenders, the general patterns could all be identified from police recorded crime data. In fact, if anything, police data tends to overestimate travel. Although previous analysis of DNA data has identified significant cross border offender movements this does not necessarily involve much travel by offenders. Forces which abut metropolitan areas are likely to have offender movements into their areas and more rural forces with tourist sites will have some longer travel offenders.

The report concludes by examining the relationship between offenders' travel to offend and victims' travel to victimisation, and how this might be analysed as part of crime pattern analysis and used for the strategic management of crime.

1.   Introduction

Background

The geography of crime is increasingly important to the work of both the police and criminologists. This is so for two reasons. First, in contemporary societies people are increasingly mobile. Such mobility could create new patterns of crime either because offenders can maraud over greater distances, or because victims travel to areas of greater risk or are more vulnerable as travellers. We need to understand, therefore, how offenders and victims come together in time and space for a crime to occur. Second, the digital technology of geographical information systems (GIS) will allow us to examine such questions much more routinely. The data to examine offender and victim movement has long existed but the methods available for doing so were laborious and expensive (see, for example, Baldwin and Bottoms, 1976). The police are very significant collectors and holders of data, but analysing and releasing the added value from that data has so far been primitive and limited. As for analysing police-held data against that held by other agencies the variations in administrative boundaries has often made this difficult. The new generation of computer analysis methods are capable of radically transforming this situation. Bringing together and interrogating large data sets is now technically routine. GIS as one new method will allow us to analyse data on spatial patterns but may also be the means for linking together different data sets at local level. These advantages will only be realisable as new computer systems become commonplace in public agencies. In the meantime the present report is an early attempt to explore how such methods may be used.

It is often assumed that because travel has become much easier in the contemporary period then offenders must be taking advantage of this fact and travelling further to commit their crimes. There is a widely held view within police forces, especially rural and urban fringe ones, that a considerable amount of high volume crime is committed by travelling, often urban offenders taking advantage of increasingly easy mobility. Many detectives have ready stories of travelling offenders invading their areas. Recently rural forces have been arguing that an increasing amount of their crime is committed by outsiders and that, since the police funding formula is largely driven by resident population, then they are not being properly resourced to deal with the problem. Furthermore, many forces have used the evidence of cross police force border crime to argue that travelling offenders are now a widespread phenomenon.

The present report examines these beliefs and attempts to identify the extent to which there is evidence to support them. It is based on research into what police recorded crime statistics and DNA records can tell us about offender travel patterns. The research mainly focuses on 'volume crime' which for this purpose was defined as burglary and TWOC (TWOC hereafter includes: Taking Without the Owners Consent, Aggravated Taking Without the Owner's Consent and Theft of a Motor Vehicle).

Previous empirical research

Most travel-to-crime research has been conducted in the United States: one important exception being the Home Office report *Tackling Cross Border Crime* (Porter, 1996). This looked at the evidence for cross border crime in the UK; that is crime which crossed police force boundaries. Its main findings were:

- the majority of police forces experienced difficulty in quantifying cross border crime;

- 10 per cent of detected crime appeared to be cross border, mostly inter-force (i.e. between adjoining forces);

- rates of cross border crime differed between forces – forces adjoining or close to large metropolitan forces and forces attracting large numbers of tourists saw rates of cross border offending of up to 23 per cent of all detected crime.

Whilst the issue of offender travel is under-researched, a number of broad findings have emerged from earlier research, particularly that conducted in North America. The most general and consistent is the fact that offenders do not appear to travel very far. With regard to burglary and car crime the following distances have been found:

Auto theft

- White (1932)   3.43 miles   Indianapolis
- Phillips (1980)   1.15 miles   Lexington-Fayette, Kentucky
- Gabor and Gottheil (1984) 1.24 miles   Ottawa

Burglary

- White (1932)   1.76 miles   Indianapolis
- Reppetto (1974)   0.5 miles   Boston and a nearby small city
- Pyle (1974) – residential   2.48 miles   Akron, Ohio
- Pyle (1974) – non-residential 2.34 miles   Akron, Ohio
- Phillips (1980)   1.05 miles   Lexington-Fayette, Kentucky
- Rhodes and Conly (1981)   1.62 miles   Washington D.C.
- Gabor and Gottheil (1984)   0.35 miles   Ottawa

The general trend is for distances to be relatively short and this does not appear to vary by time of day or time of year. It is also worth noting that Pyle (1974) found travel to burglary the longest of the offences they examined whereas Gabor and Gottheil (1984) found it to be the shortest. Another general finding has been that travel-to-crime increases with the age of the offender (Phillips, 1980; Baldwin and Bottoms, 1976; Davidson, 1984; Reppetto, 1974; Reiss and Farrington, 1991).

With regard to gender and distance most studies have concentrated on male offenders and so there are no clear findings with regard to gender and distance. Much of the research carried out in the US has been interested in the issue of race. The general finding is that black offenders travel shorter distances than white offenders and that offending is intra-, not inter-racial (see, for example, Rand, (1986); Rengert and Wasilchick, (1985); Phillips, (1980) and Carter and Hill, (1979).

Reasons for travel

Explanations of the movement patterns identified by empirical research have been dominated by the issue of 'rationality'. In simple terms this focuses on whether we explain travel-to-crime as a consequence of instrumentally rational searching by highly motivated offenders, or as a result of affectually rational, opportunistic behaviour committed whilst 'potential' offenders are pursuing their day-to-day routine activities. This simple dichotomy is complicated by the possibility that the same offender may at different times straddle the categories. Furthermore, it could be that, say, domestic burglary is generally committed following instrumentally rational reasoning, whilst TWOC is mainly carried out for affectually rational reasons. Even within a single crime category, such as car theft, there could be different travel-to-crime explanations for 'joyriding' and stealing a car to 'ring' or 'chop'.

The theories produced by previous research do not point to one single explanation of offender mobility (for a fuller review see Bottoms and Wiles, 1999). The problem with the existing studies is that although they suggest explanations these are often simply hypotheses which appear to plausibly fit the facts, but are not always backed up by empirical research findings. Furthermore, such hypothecated explanations are often embedded in broader, master theories of criminal or general social action. For example, instrumental explanations of offender's travel are embedded in broad theories of rational choice and have been related to crime prevention notions of target hardening. There is nothing wrong with such an approach (indeed, it is a necessary aspect of explanations which operate at different levels of generality) except that sometimes empirical investigation has been limited within a broader theory and so is not capable of arbitrating between explanations which belong to different master theories.

In spite of this limitation there are a number of central issues which emerge for further examination:

- To what extent do offenders instrumentally travel as part of a search pattern for suitable targets?

- To what extent do offenders travel as part of their routine non-criminal activities and then within those patterns commit crimes?

- Are there any systematic differences in travel-to-crime patterns between different types of offender or different types of offences?

- Are there different travel-to-crime patterns for different types of geographical area?

- How do all of these relate to victim's travel-to-crime patterns?

Answers to these questions will provide better grounded explanations of offenders' travel and also hold out the possibility of providing models of offender and victim mobility which can be used for crime pattern analysis for the management and prevention of crime.

Structure of the report

This report is structured as follows:

- Section 2 outlines the data examined and the methods employed in the production of this study;

- Section 3 presents our findings based upon recorded crime data for Sheffield and North Yorkshire;

- Section 4 presents findings from an analysis of the Forensic Science Service's DNA database;

- Section 5 reports on findings from a series of interviews with burglars and car thieves from the Sheffield area; and,

- Section 6 sets out the conclusions and crime management recommendations of this report.

2. Data and methods

The research uses data from two police forces, from the Police National Computer (PNC) and from interviews carried out with a stratified sample of recently convicted burglary and TWOC offenders. These sources of data rely on information about, and from, convicted offenders. It could be argued that since the police generally only clear up about a fifth of offences recorded by them, and these include 'clear ups' not based on a court conviction, then the data may be heavily contaminated by policing practices rather than reflecting general offender behaviour. This is a perennial problem with many studies of offenders. A defence of the use of police data is that offenders known to the police are generally the more prolific and persistent: certainly the interview sample had this bias. The findings of the present study, therefore, may be biased towards the behaviour patterns of the more persistent and prolific offenders. However, from the point of view of informing policing practice this may be an advantage. Resources were not available to find offenders not known to the police to interview[1]. However, the National DNA database was used to look for travel patterns where the offenders involved were not necessarily known to the police.

Police recorded crime data

The police recorded crime data was provided by South Yorkshire and North Yorkshire police forces. South Yorkshire Police provided a data set of all offences, offenders and complainants for the city of Sheffield for 1995. This amounted to 70,163 offences, 54,564 victims (complainants) and 8,109 offenders. North Yorkshire Police provided similar data for the whole of the force area for 1997 and gave data on 49,090 offences, 53,949 complainants and 10,463 offenders. Both these sets of data were geocoded using a MapInfo Geographical Information System (GIS)[2].

A GIS is simply a computer programme which enables the geographical location of any data to be mapped using x and y co-ordinates and then to be analysed against topographical or other digitised maps, or other data sets which are also geographically referenced. The offences were geocoded by where they occurred, complainants by their home address, and offenders by their home address. This was done by using computer software which automatically geocodes any location which has a recognisable address,

---

1   This is expensive because it either involves using a general population sample to find the (relative) few who have committed burglary or TWOC, or snowballing from known offenders in the hope of contacting non-known offenders.

2   MapInfo was chosen for its ease of use but any other GIS would have been equally suitable.

although this produced accurate coding in less than half of the offences. Much of the data had to be geocoded by hand, such as where an offence had occurred in a park and therefore had no 'address' as such. A proportion had to be geocoded to the nearest postcode or approximate postcode level[3].

The advantage of geocoded data for this study was threefold. First, it allowed distances between a large number of geographical locations to be measured very quickly using x/y co-ordinates. Throughout this paper distance measures are all 'straight-line' (i.e. the shortest distance between two points). Some researchers (often American, where many cities are laid out in a regular grid pattern) have used other measures of distance such as 'cab route distance' to try and reflect the most likely route between two points. However, in many British cities it is not always easy to identify one likely route between two points and therefore the straight-line distance is used here as the best available standard measure. The data was analysed with particular reference to the distance between the home address of known offenders and the place of offence commission (offender movements[4]), and the home address of complainants, all of which could be linked via each offence's unique crime number. Secondly, it also meant that underlying socio-demographic data could easily be linked to the crime data. Finally, by geocoding the data a flexible geography was achieved so that the analysis was not limited by the boundaries of police beats or basic command units.

Data from South and North Yorkshire was used so as to compare offender movements in a large post-industrial city with those in small towns and rural areas. Time constraints prevented geocoding another large dataset from another force area covering smaller industrial towns and different kinds of rural areas. As geocoding becomes routine for police data then the kind of analysis reported here will be able to be quickly and easily replicated elsewhere.

PNC recorded crime data

One problem with using individual police force data is that whilst it includes information about offences committed in its force area by offenders from elsewhere (imported offenders), it does not include data about offenders who live in the force area but who commit their offences elsewhere (exported offenders). In order to examine this problem Police National

---

3   Offender and victim data is relatively straightforward to geocode as it generally contains a recognisable address, offence data is slightly more problematic as offences such as TWOC, violence, robbery, etc. often take place away from a residential/business address. Less than 1 per cent of offenders had to be excluded from the analysis due to the records recording 'no fixed abode'.

4   Throughout we refer to offender movements; this is because each offender can be involved in more than one offence and one offence can be committed by more than one offender.

Computer (PNC) records were used. The details of all convicted offenders for the period July 1995 – June 1996 who gave a Sheffield home address but who on arrest had been taken to a police station outside the city were extracted[5]. This gave details of a further 2534 offender movements by Sheffield-based offenders. Whilst the home addresses of these offenders were geocoded it was not possible to precisely geocode the offence location for two reasons. First, the data only came with police station codes for the offence and, second, digitised maps for the whole of the country would be required. However, it was possible to calculate approximate distances travelled and for these longer journeys these were quite adequate for present purposes. This is explained further in Chapter 4.

DNA database 'hits'

The National DNA database was established in 1995 by the Forensic Science Service (FSS). Any police force can send DNA samples to the FSS for analysi[6] . Each sample sent is given a unique reference on FSS's database and a code to indicate which police station has sent the sample. Each sample is automatically compared with all other samples held on the database. Samples relate either to a stain found at a crime scene or a DNA sample taken from a crime suspect; the latter are taken from suspects arrested for recordable offences and are deleted if no conviction follows. In the period January 1995 to December 1997 a total of 398,147 samples were received and 229,355 retained. The vast majority of samples related to either burglary or auto crime.

Data on all cases between June 1997 and December 1997 were provided, where comparison showed that the same person was responsible for two stains or DNA samples and where the two samples had different police station codes. This gave a data base where there was prima facie evidence of offender mobility, although there was no information on where the offender lived. The data set consisted of 7,820 matched samples of which 6,246 related to burglary and 1,133 to auto crime.[7]

---

5 Unfortunately PNC data could not be provided for the whole of 1995 because of the recent implementation of the new Phoenix system, so we took the closest possible dates.

6 One problem with this database is that since police forces have to pay for each sample they submit then the rate at which samples are sent may not reflect police forces populations or crime rates. See further comments later in the report.

7 The remainder were: 33 ABH/GBH; 64 rapes and other sexual offences; 75 robberies; 111 thefts; and 112 criminal damage cases, with the remainder being unclassified.

Offender interviews

One potential weakness with the methodology described so far is that offender addresses in police records may be inaccurate, or out of date, and more generally the records cannot provide more qualitative information about why offenders travel to crimes in the way shown by police data. In order to gather such qualitative data interviews were conducted with a sample of 70 Sheffield-based convicted offenders. This sample was stratified as set out in Table 2.1, in order to examine whether there were any identifiable differences between burglars and TWOCers; between different age offenders; and between apparent travellers and non-travellers. The offence type for each offender was taken from the index offence for which they had just been sentenced. Travellers were defined as those offenders who in the offence for which they had just been sentenced had travelled more than 2 miles. In addition, a special sub-group of 'professional' offenders were identified by South Yorkshire Police to see whether they had a different movement patter. They were drawn from the police list of the most prolific 25 burglars and 25 TWOCers in the city.

The offenders were mainly interviewed whilst in prison immediately after sentence although some of the youngest offenders were not in custody at the time of interview (because of the much lower rates of imprisonment for juvenile offenders). This was done mainly to ensure that the interviews were completed within the research timescale, but does mean that those interviewed were a group of the more persistent and serious offenders. The offenders interviewed were simply taken sequentially from those who were sentenced in Sheffield after the start date and fitted the criteria for each cell in the interview matrix, until each cell was complete. In the event it was not possible to identify enough TWOCers aged over 25 and so this group was dropped leaving 60 offenders (35 burglars and 25 TWOCers). The inability to find older TWOCers is, however, consistent with the findings reported below on the relationship between offending and age.

Table 2.1: **Offender Interview Sample Matrix**

Age	Burglars		TWOCers	
	travel	non-travel	travel	non-travel
< 18	5	5	5	5
18-25	5	5	5	5
>25	5	5	5	5
Professionals	5	-	5	-
Totals	20	15	20	15

3.

Offender travel within Sheffield

Travel-to-crime distances for offences committed in the City of Sheffield (Table 3.1) are fairly short and are similar to the findings of previous research. The great majority of the offenders are young males, with only shoplifting producing a sizeable proportion of female offenders (44%).

The data in Table 3.1 counts all movements made by offenders, including joint offending. However, for all offences carried out by an offender acting alone (1132 offences), the average journey to offend was 1.73 miles. For the 166 offences carried out by two or more offenders, the average journey to offend for the co-offenders making the shortest journey was 1.35 miles, and for the co-offender making the longest journey it was 3.17 miles. If we take solo journeys, and the shortest distance travelled to a joint offence, the average journey overall falls to 1.68 miles. For TWOC, the same process reduces the average journey to crime from 2.36 miles to 2.10 miles.

Table 3.1: *Average distance travelled and age of offender: for selected offences within Sheffield, 1995*

Offence	Average Distance (miles)	Average Age (years)	Number of Cases
All Offences	1.93	22.5	1179
A.B.H.	1.49	25.9	607
Shoplifting	2.51	22.5	2065
Theft from Vehicle	1.97	19.2	984
Domestic Burglary	1.88	21.3	1401
Non-Domestic Burglary	1.83	21.8	983
TWOC	2.36	18.8	1326

One of the most consistent findings from previous research has been that young offenders do not travel as far as older offenders. Table 3.2 shows that more recent findings for Sheffield suggest that this relationship may be changing.

Table 3.2:   Age v Distance Correlation Coefficients: Selected Offences, Sheffield, 1995

Offender Movements	Age v Distance Correlation
All Offences	-0.0912***
A.B.H.	-0.0790*
Shoplifting	-0.1699***
Theft from a Vehicle	+0.0910*
Domestic Burglary	+0.0327 ns
Non-Domestic Burglary	+0.0446 ns
TWOC	-0.0488*

Notes
1.   *** significant at the 0.1 per cent level; ** significant at the 1 per cent level; significant at the 5 per cent level; ns not significant
2.   All the above correlations based upon Pearson Correlation Coefficient 1 tailed test using actual distances

Only theft from a motor vehicle now shows a statistically significant positive correlation between age and distance to crime. Yet car ownership has increased and so the need to travel to find a vehicle to victimise ought, if anything, to be less not more. Burglary shows no correlation and TWOC shows a statistically significant negative correlation. Therefore, for Sheffield-based offenders offending in the city, there is no longer a positive correlation between travel-to-crime and age.

Sheffield recorded crime datea 1966 and 1995: changes in travel

There is a definite change in travel-to-crime patterns in Sheffield in 1966 with regard to burglary and auto crime (Baldwin and Bottoms, 1976) compared with 1995 as set out in Tables 3.3 and 3.4.

Table 3.3: Sheffield offenders: burglary, 1966 and 1995[8]

Distance	% All breaking & burglary		% Offenders 10-15 years		% Offenders 16-25 years		% Offenders 26 and above	
	1966	1995	1966	1995	1966	1995	1966	1995
< 1 mile	54.4	41.3	75.6	62.2	43.3	39.6	42.3	36.1
1 – 1.9 miles	20.4	20.4	15.6	15.9	21.0	19.8	27.1	25.2
2 – 2.9 miles	11.3	16.5	3.4	8.1	16.2	17.3	14.1	18.4
3+ miles	13.9	21.8	5.4	13.8	19.5	23.3	16.5	20.2

Notes
1. Breaking offences, 1966 (n=417).
2. Non-domestic and domestic burglary, 1995 (n=2384).
3. Spearman rank correlation coefficients based on distance bands for 1966 data:

    1966 Breakings: age v distance   +0.2839 ***
    1995 Burglaries: age v distance   +0.0913 ***
    *** significant at the 0.1 per cent level

Table 3.4: Sheffield offenders: car crime

Distance	% All TWOC & TDA		% Offenders 10-15 years		% Offenders 16-25 years		% Offenders 26 and above	
	1966	1995	1966	1995	1966	1995	1966	1995
< 1 mile	45.0	27.1	75.6	28.1	39.1	26.7	38.7	28.6
1-1.9 miles	18.3	23.9	12.2	22.3	19.5	24.9	19.4	16.9
>2-2.9 miles	13.7	17.8	8.1	17.3	14.1	18.0	19.4	16.9
3+ miles	23.0	31.3	4.1	32.4	27.3	30.4	22.5	37.7

Notes
1. TDA, 1966 (n=300).
2. Twoc, theft of motor vehicle and aggravated vehicle theft, 1995 (n=1326).
3. Spearman rank correlation coefficients:
    1966 TDAs   age v distance   +0.2250 ***
    1995 TWOC,   etc.: age v distance   +0.0063 ns
    *** = sig>=0.1 per cent

As Tables 3.3 and 3.4 show the difference between how far young and old offenders travel to commit crimes is much less clear than thirty years ago.[9] Distances travelled by offenders within the city have generally increased and the old relationship between age and distance

8   For the 1966 data each offender's average distance was counted (i.e. total distance travelled divided by number of offences) for the 1995 data each journey made by an offender was counted separately. We tested the 1966 method on the 1995 data and found it made no significant difference to the results.

9   Unfortunately the 1966 data was collected in age bands only and so we can not directly compare age v distance. This results in the slightly changed correlation coefficients for the 1995 data.

is breaking down. The most likely explanation for this change is that, in addition to increased access to legitimate car use (see Table 5.2), increased theft of vehicles has provided greater mobility and, as Table 3.1 shows, that is a young man's offence. What remains to be explained is whether the availability of a stolen car leads to greater exploration of the city generally and hence greater mobility of offenders as new areas are discovered.

Sheffield recorded crime data: offender movements into and out of the city

Police force recorded offence and offender data will always give the appearance that a force is a net importer of offenders because the data will include information about offences committed in the force area by those who live elsewhere, but not about those who live in the force area but commit their offences elsewhere. For example, the 1995 data for Sheffield showed that of cleared up offences, 12,538 were committed by offenders living in Sheffield but 1,849 by offenders living elsewhere (13.6% of all offenders involved in cleared up offences in the city). In order to correct this impression of Sheffield being an importer of offenders, the details of all convicted offenders for the period July 1995 – June 1996 who gave a Sheffield home address but who on arrest had been taken to a police station outside the city were extracted from the Police National Computer (PNC).

This gave details of a further 2,534 offender movements by Sheffield-based offenders. This amounted to 2,534 offender movements out of the city and 2,127 movements in[10], making Sheffield a net exporter of known offenders. The offences committed by these imported and exported offenders are different from those who commit their offences near to home. In particular, offenders moving into Sheffield are likely to commit shoplifting offences. Of all journeys into the city which end in an offence almost half (46%) are shoplifting. Whilst shoplifting is slightly more common as an offence amongst journeys to offend out of the city, compared with journeys wholly within the city (23% compared with 19%), there is nevertheless not a great deal of difference for Sheffield-based offenders. The relatively straightforward reason for this is that Sheffield with a large city centre, the giant Meadowhall shopping mall on the edge of town, and many smaller retail parks provides plenty of opportunities for shoplifting offences both for residents and outsiders.

---

10 Being the offender movements of the 1849 non-Sheffield offenders recorded by South Yorkshire Police.

Table 3.5:   *Origin of imported offenders and destination of exported offenders – Sheffield*

Place	No. of offenders out of city		No. of offenders into city	
	(%)	(n)	(%)	(n)
Rotherham	21	(528)	46	(981)
N.E. Derbyshire	18	(455)	5	(102)
Doncaster	8	(210)	9	(191)
Barnsley	6	(156)	11	(235)
Leeds	3	(64)	2	(51)
London	3	(64)		(25)
Skegness	2	(52)	0	(0)
Worksop	2	(48)	2	(51)
Other	38	(957)	23	(492)
Total	2534		2127	

Table 3.5 shows the destination of exported offenders and the origin of imported offenders. For both exports and imports over 50 per cent of movements are between Sheffield and places closely linked with the city (57% of exports and 73% of imports). As can be seen the strongest single link is between Sheffield and Rotherham. This is unsurprising since Sheffield and Rotherham share a long boundary which in many places is effectively meaningless as the two places merge: industry and employment has traditionally been shared in the Don Valley; Sheffield has long attracted shoppers from Rotherham; and the new Meadowhall shopping mall, whilst in Sheffield, is right on the border between the two places.

Both imported and exported offender movements differ from the within city offender movements in the type of offences which dominate (see Table 6)[11] and their direction of travel. For example, Sheffielders visit Skegness, but few visits occur in the opposite direction; hence the crime pattern[12]. The same pattern can be seen with places such as Barnsley and North East Derbyshire: the former producing more visits to Sheffield, for shopping, entertainment and work purposes, whereas Sheffielders tend to head towards Derbyshire for leisure. The 'other' section in both of the above categories showed no particular pattern, although there was a tendency for movements out of Sheffield to be towards tourist-type places whereas movements in tended to be from other urban areas. It can be surmised that Sheffield offender's movements out of the city were mainly a by-product of leisure/holiday trips.

11 Imports, in particular, differ because of the level of shoplifting by non-Sheffielders at Meadowhall
12 Skegness has long been the 'Sheffield resort' a development which came with the railways but has endured to the extent that the Sheffield Star is available in Skegness throughout the summer months and Sheffield United play a pre-season friendly against Skegness Town each summer.

Examining the distances travelled out of Sheffield to offend, not only is the average distance travelled not very great but even this is distorted by a few long distance travellers, as can be seen by comparing the average (mean) with the mid-point of the distances travelled (median) in Table 3.6. The greater distances recorded for out of city violence is because many of the offences are committed at seaside resorts, whereas each of the other medians fall directly within Sheffield's normal day-to-day sphere of mobility.

Table 3.6:   Average distance by offence (miles)

	Distance: miles		
	Sheffield – based offender movements)	Mean out of City	Median out of City
All Offences	6.86	35.05	18
A.B.H.	3.78	55.16	48.5
Shoplifting	7.93	34.52	18
Theft from vehicle	3.37	22.67	9
Domestic burglary	4.66	31.92	16
Non-domestic burglary	5.94	32.85	18
TWOC etc.	7.11	30.81	11

To an extent the idea of increasing travel can be confounded by comparing the origin of those offending in Sheffield in 1966 and 1995. As Table 3.7 shows there has been no change in the proportion of cleared up offences in the city committed by residents and non-residents over a thirty year period.

Table 3.7:   Place of residence of those offending in Sheffield: 1966 and 1995

Place of Residence	1966		1995	
	(%)	(n)	(%)	(n)
Sheffield	85.9	(984)	85.6	(6,910)
Non-Sheffield	14.1	(162)	14.4	(1,163)

The impact of Meadowhall

Meadowhall is a very large out of town shopping mall built on the site of what was the centre of Sheffield's steel industry, adjacent to the M1 motorway and on the border with Rotherham. It is interesting because it is the largest attractor of visitors to the city and also the main attractor of imported offenders. Of all offender movements into the city almost half (41%) result in offending at Meadowhall; and of these 80 per cent are shoplifting offences. However, there is no real evidence of long journeys to offend at Meadowhall, 56 per cent of all non-Sheffielders convicted of shoplifting at Meadowhall are from adjoining Rotherham. A similar pattern holds with victims of crime at Meadowhall. Of all visitors to the city who become victims of crime in Sheffield, 11 per cent are victimised at Meadowhall (mainly car crime victimisations) the highest count of any place in the city. This compares with only 2 per cent of all victimisations of Sheffielders at Meadowhall.

Recorded crime data: Sheffield compared with North Yorkshire

The crime patterns of all places are, of course, to some extent unique. It was necessary to explore how far the patterns for Sheffield were generalisable elsewhere. This was investigated by looking at patterns of crime in North Yorkshire.

North Yorkshire police force area is a mixture of medium and small towns together with rural areas. To compare with Sheffield patterns, the crime patterns for the City of York and Hambleton District, a largely rural area were studied. The patterns for burglary and TWOC are shown in Tables 3.8 and 3.9.

Table 3.8: **Burglary and TWOC: mean age of offenders and distance travelled to offend**

Place	Burglary (mean)		TWOC (mean)	
	Distance (miles)	Age	Distance (miles)	Age
York	0.98	20.6	0.99	17.0
Hambleton	1.68	18.2	2.27	20.0
Sheffield	1.80	21.5	2.32	18.8

Note:
1. NB distances in York and Hambleton include all N Yorks offenders whether they lived in the study areas or not.

Table 3.9: Origin of burglary and TWOC known offenders York, Hambleton and Sheffield

Origin of offenders	% Burglary			% TWOC		
	York	Hamb	Sheff	York	Hamb	Sheff
Within LA district	90	62	97	84	37	95
Within county	5	1	2	4	0	3
Outside county	5	37	1	12	63	2
Total	279	159	3314	151	57	1735

The City of York has a similar pattern to Sheffield, albeit with much less crime (approximately half the Sheffield rate). Most offending is very local and carried out by young males; in fact the offending by York-based offenders is even more geographically localised than offending within Sheffield.

Hambleton, with a very low crime rate, has a very different pattern, especially with regard to TWOC. Offenders from outside the district are much more important, but in the context of relatively few offences in absolute terms. Hambleton's northern boundary abuts part of the southern boundary of Cleveland and the vast majority of these offenders are from nearby higher crime areas to the north. In some ways this represents a similar pattern to Sheffield offenders' movement into North East Derbyshire. In both cases the rural areas attract people from the neighbouring urban areas for broadly leisure and recreational reasons, some of whom then either get to know the area for possible offending or coincidentally offend whilst there.

An interesting pattern of offence location is found when travel into Hambleton associated with theft from motor vehicle offences is examined. Offenders from outside North Yorkshire come from higher crime areas to the north (Cleveland and Tyne and Wear provide the origin for 53 out of the 54 offender movements). However, half of all offender movements into Hambleton end on the A1 road: not just close to the road but actually at service stations. This is in direct contrast to the 62 offender movements originating in the county where none of the offence locations are on the A1, but instead are generally in the small towns close to the offender's home. For North Yorkshire offenders offending in the county the average distance travelled is 2.5 miles but for the offender movements wholly within Hambleton District (58 out of 62) this drops to 1.7 miles.

In a sense these findings are not surprising, both groups of offenders are offending in areas where they, and others, probably perceive they belong. One of the characteristics of service stations is that they are mass spaces where anyone has a claim to be and where the majority of people at any given time will probably be from outside North Yorkshire. As an outside offender this is probably the most rational place to offend: there are no 'strangers', access in and out is easy and quick, and travellers visiting a service station tend to leave valuables (often conveniently packed) in their car. This pattern is not replicated for either burglary or TWOC: burglary because there are few opportunities at such locations (motorway services tend to be open for 24 hours), and TWOCs probably because cars are left unattended for relatively short periods of time and it is much quicker (generally) to steal from a car than to steal the car itself.

At the general level of offender movements it is possible to illustrate how North Yorkshire differs from Sheffield by examining the origin of offender movements which result in offending in the two areas. Whilst North Yorkshire imports a much higher proportion of offenders than Sheffield, nevertheless over three-quarters of offender movements still begin and end in the county (see Table 3.10 below). Furthermore, as noted above, distance travelled by local offenders is, if anything, even less than in Sheffield. Offenders imported into North Yorkshire are predominately from the surrounding urban areas and may not, of course, have travelled any significant distance (see Chapter 4). Given that parts of North Yorkshire are international tourist destinations then one might expect greater victimisation of outsiders in such places. Comparing Sheffield TWOCs whose victims were from the Sheffield travel-to-work area with York TWOCs whose victims were from North Yorkshire, shows that in both cases this makes up 90 per cent of all victims.

Table 3.10: Comparing the Origin of Offenders in Sheffield (1995) and North Yorkshire (1997)

Offender Movements	Sheffield		North Yorkshire	
	(%)	(n)	(%)	(n)
Within Area	87	(14234)	76	(11872)
Originating Outside Area	13	(2127)	24	(3670)
Total	16361		15542	

Travel within Sheffield: different area patterns

The discussion so far has focused on the general situation with regard to Sheffield. Very different travel patterns emerge in different types of small residential areas. A consistent pattern in the Sheffield data is that the offence rate in most residential neighbourhoods of the city is driven by the local offender rate. This can be illustrated by looking at patterns of offending and victimisation in a series of residential districts. The findings with regard to these areas are set out in Tables 3.12 and 3.13 and the neighbourhoods are described in Table 3.11.

The lifestyle analysis utilised is GB Profiler developed by Professor Stan Openshaw of Leeds University. *[It can be downloaded from http://www.geog.leeds.ac.uk/software/gbprofiles/]*

1   *Struggling; Multi-ethnic Areas – Pensioners & single parents – high unemployment – LA rented flats*

2   *Struggling; Council Tenants – Blue collar families & single parents – LA rented terraces*

3   *Struggling; Less Prosperous Pensioner Areas – Retired blue collar residents – LA rented semis*

4   *Struggling; Multi-ethnic Areas; Less Prosperous Private Renters – Young blue collar families with children – privately renting terraces & bedsits*

5   *Aspiring; Academic Centres & Student Areas – Young educated white collar singles & couples – privately rented bedsits & flats*

6   *Aspiring; Young Married Suburbia – Young well-off blue collar couples & families – mixed tenure terraces*

7   *Climbing; Well-Off Suburban Areas – Young white collar couples & families – buying semis & detached houses*

8   *Established; Rural Farming Communities – Mature well-off self-employed couples & pensioners – owning or privately renting large detached houses*

Looking at offenders offending in these areas it is found, not surprisingly, that offenders travel the greatest distance to offend in the low offender/offence rate areas – on average over 3.5 miles (see Table 3.12). The shortest distances to offend are all found in the high offence/offender areas: again confirming the earlier finding that most offender travel is short-scale. Equally interesting is the fact that the issue of victim travel is at least as important as offender travel for the more affluent areas. In both the very high status areas (A and B) almost 50 per cent of victimisations takes place outside the area of residence compared with about 10 per cent in area G which has a high offender and offence rate (see Table 3.13). Partly this is due to different types of victimisation: burglary in the high victimisation/offence areas and car crime against the middle classes. The important point is that the middle classes do not become victims just because offenders travel but because they themselves move around the city as part of their routines. The issue of the relationship between offender and victim travel is returned to in Chapter 6.

Note   For definitions in Table 3.11 of 'high', 'medium' and 'low', see footnote 26

Table 3.11: Sheffield neighbourhoods: characteristics

Area	Characteristics	Main Lifestyle Categories	Recorded crime pattern
A	An exclusive middle class suburb on the edge of the city, 6 miles from the city centre.	8 and 9	low offender low offence rates
B	An exclusive middle class suburb, 2.5 miles from the city centre.	9 and 10	low offender low offender rates
C	A working class/lower middle class suburb, 6 miles from the city centre, mainly consisting of owner occupied housing but with a substantial minority of council housing.	3 and 7 and 10	medium offence medium offender rates
D	An area of turn of the century terraced, owner occupied housing, with a substantial minority of private rented student accommodation and a mixed class structure; it is 1.5 miles from the city centre.	5 and 6	medium offence medium offender rates
E	A terraced housing area with a substantial student population but more middle class structure than Area D; generally considered a desirable residential suburb 1 mile from the city centre.	5 and 6	high offence low offender rates
F	Three fairly small and deprived council estates 3 miles from the city centre; one of the estates has long had a very poor reputation in the city.	2	high offender high offence rates
G	A council estate 2 miles from the city centre; it has a poor reputation in the city and is one of its most deprived neighbourhoods.	2	high offender high offence rates
H	An area 1 mile from the city centre with a sizeable ethnic minority population (about 25%) mainly Asian but also Afro-Caribbean. A deprived area which has a poor reputation in the city. The housing is a mix of modern public housing (mainly flats) cheap owner occupied terraces and private renting, some in multi-occupation.	1, 2 and 4	high offender high offence rates
I	An area of mainly system-built 1960s housing with the shortest waiting list of any public housing in the city. A mile from the city centre, the area is characterised by poverty and a poor reputation.	1 and 2	high offender high offence rates

Table 3.12: Travel to offend in selected residential areas: Sheffield 1995

Area	Total offender movements in area	From within area (%) (n)	From elsewhere in Sheffield (%) (n)	From prison address[13] (%) (n)	From outside Sheffield (%) (n)	Average distance of Sheffield-based offenders (miles)
A	153	21.6 (33)	66.0 (101)	11.5 (18)	2.6 (4)	3.96
B	117	6.8 (8)	64.1 (75)	18.8 (22)	10.6 (12)	3.51
C	282	37.9 (107)	43.6 (123)	5.7 (16)	9.2 (26)	2.85
D	123	12.2 (15)	73.2 (90)	4.1 (5)	10.6 (13)	2.32
E	332	2.7 (9)	65.4 (217)	28.6 (95)	3.3 (11)	2.27
F	440	59.3 (261)	35.7 (157)	0.5 (2)	4.5 (20)	0.81
G	378	54.2 (205)	41.8 (158)	0.8 (3)	3.2 (12)	0.97
H	422	47.4 (200)	41.8 (178)	5.5 (23)	3.2 (12)	1.09
I	348	53.7 (187)	38.5 (134)	2.6 (9)	5.2 (18)	0.77

---

13 For the great majority of these, the last known residential address was in Sheffield.

Table 3.13: Distance to victimisation by home area: Sheffield 1995

Area	Resident Complainants	In area victimisation (%) (n)	Out of area victimisation (%) (n)	Average distance: home to victimisation
A	984	52.2 (514)	47.8 (470)	2.01 miles
B	933	54.8 (511)	45.2 (422)	1.73 miles
C	1986	73.3 (1456)	26.7 (530)	1.35 miles
D	694	69.0 (479)	31.0 (215)	0.47 miles
E	1043	68.4 (713)	31.6 (330)	0.55 miles
F	1225	84.4 (1034)	16.6 (191)	0.31 miles
G	1243	89.0 (1106)	11 (137)	0.23 miles
H	1415	84.5 (1195)	15.5 (220)	0.30 miles

4:   DNA database analysis

The data

The analysis of the Forensic Science Service (FSS) database included 7,820 cases (covering June - December 1997) where DNA comparison showed that the same person was responsible for two stains or DNA samples taken from an offender, and where the two samples had different police station codes. The FSS only maintains a limited central data base and the only geographical reference this includes is the code of the police station which submitted the DNA sample. The analysis therefore makes the assumption that the submitting police station code is a reasonable proxy for the geographical location of a stain site or an offender's place of residence. The DNA data is thus not so geographically specific as either the police data or interview data and cannot be used to examine short distance movement. However, it is adequate to look at offender movement which crosses between divisions within the same force and between forces. Table 4.1 shows the breakdown of these matches by offence type and Table 4.2 sets out the extent of geographical movements involved in these matches.

Table 4.1:   DNA 'movement' matches by offence type

Offence	(%)	(n)	% 1997 Recorded Crime Data
Domestic Burglary	35	(2765)	11
Non-Domestic Burglary	45	(3481)	11
Autocrime	14	(1133)	24
Other	6	(441)	54
All Offences	7820		100

Police forces who submit samples to the FSS have to pay for their analysis and match searches. One question this raises is how far the DNA sample is in any sense nationally representative. Scotland has been excluded from the analysis because the Scottish forces submitted very few samples compared to those in England and Wales. Submissions and matches by the English and Welsh forces were found to closely correlate with the amount of overall crime at force level.[14] The DNA database, therefore, is broadly comparable with

14 The correlation between DNA matches by force and recorded crime by force was +0.9570 which is significant at the 0.1 per cent level (Pearson Correlation Coefficient).

levels of recorded crime by force and so is broadly representative of *levels* of crime in England and Wales. However, the database is unrepresentative in terms of offence type, with burglary dominating to a much greater extent than for recorded crime nationally (see Table 4.1). This difference reflects the kind of cases for which the police are most likely to recover DNA stains and the fact that DNA analysis is as much used evidentially to help secure convictions as it is for detection purposes. This difference in offence types must be borne in mind in the discussion that follows.

Results

The DNA database provided 7820 'movement hits' for the period June – December 1997, out of a total of 15536 hits where DNA samples matched. However, a number of hits had to be excluded (most often because the releva police division could be not identified) leaving a total of 7745 movement hits and 15451 hits overall. This produces the pattern of matches set out in Table 4.2.

Table 4.2:   DNA matches by inter-divisional movement.

DNA Matches	(%)	(n)	% Movement Matches
Non-Adjoining Force	7	(1067)	14
Adjoining Force	7	(1144)	15
Within Force (Movement - different division)	36	(5534)	71
Within Force (No Movement - same division)	50	(7706)	n/a
Total	15451	100	

As can be seen the vast majority of matches are within force, and half of all matches are within the same police division. Even examining matches involving apparent movement shows that the overwhelming majority are within force. Furthermore, movement between adjoining divisions (whether this also involves cross force boundary movement or not) could involve no more than crossing a road. The importance of these results are that they confirm the findings based upon police data and the interviews (see Chapter 5), that the majority of offender movements are relatively short. Also, given the over-representation of burglary and car crime in the DNA database, it is apparent that the offence types which form the main element of this study (volume crime) appear to be localised phenomena.

However, as found in the comparison of Sheffield with North Yorkshire, and the comparison of suburbs within Sheffield, there are important differences by type of area. In particular, it is evident that there are two broad patterns within the DNA database: urban versus suburban and rural[15]. Forces with 80 per cent or more of hits solely within force included South Yorkshire, Northumbria, Greater Manchester and West Midlands; the only non-Metropolitan force with such a high proportion of internal hits is Avon and Somerset, which includes a significant metropolitan area. The forces with over 40 per cent of hits involving an adjacent force included West Mercia, North Yorkshire (both rural); and Cheshire, Surrey, Essex, Hertfordshire and Warwickshire (all suburban)[16]. Forces where over 33 per cent of matches were with a non-adjacent force included: Dyfed, Suffolk, North Wales, Norfolk, Lincolnshire, Cumbria (all rural) and Sussex (suburban). Whilst these individual force findings might suggest that rural forces show more non-adjacent matches and suburban forces adjacent matches, this does not appear to be the case in Table 4.3 which sets out the broad pattern for these groups. It is apparent that the main difference between the forces is that those which have hits with adjoining forces abut metropolitan areas whilst those with non-adjacent matches are tourist areas (findings that appear to confirm Porter's (1996) cross border crime study).

Table 4.3:   Matches by type of force[17]

Type of force	Non-Adjoining Force		Adjoining Force		Within Force (Movement: between Divisions)		Within Force (Non-Movement: within same Division)	
	(%)	(n)	(%)	(n)	(%)	(n)	(%)	(n)
Rural	20	(289)	18	(254)	29	(411)	33	(462)
Suburban	17	(446))	17	(465)	25	(668)	41	(1082)
Urban	10	(396)	9	(349)	46	(1866)	35	(1412)
Metropolitan Police	11	(255)	12	(282)	73	(1688)	4	(101)

15 The categorisation of forces is based on HMIC's 'Most Similar Forces' groups.

16 The City of London force also shows over 40 per cent of hits in an adjoining force but this is something of a special case.

17 It should be noted that this table will tend to exaggerate movement between forces. For example, a matched pair of samples in Greater Manchester will count as one match, whereas a matched pair of samples with one match in Essex and one match in Cambridgeshire will count twice, once for each force.

18 In this table rural forces are: Lincolnshire, Norfolk, Wiltshire, Devon and Cornwall, West Mercia, Derbyshire and Cambridgeshire. Suburban forces are: Essex, Kent, Bedfordshire, Sussex, Hampshire, Thames Valley, Warwickshire and Avon and Somerset. Urban forces are: West Yorkshire, Greater Manchester, South Yorkshire and West Midlands.

The contrast between the London pattern and the rest of urban Britain can perhaps be explained by the extensive public transport network in the capital and also the mobility of the population both in terms of residential mobility and mobility for work and leisure. Similar evidence of offending-related movement was found in the Home Office study of *Operation Eagle Eye* with displacement around the underground system in response to policing operations (Stockdale and Gresham, 1998).

The DNA matches allowed an examination of movement at the level of police divisions. This was done using Greater Manchester because it had a large number of hits and good connections to potentially attractive targets in adjoining forces such as Cheshire and Derbyshire. The overall matches for GMP are set out in Table 4.4.

Table 4.4: DNA matches for Greater Manchester Police

Within force	81	(934)
Adjoining force	8	(96)
Non-adjoining force	11	(122)
Total	1152	

This shows that the vast majority of matches are within the GMP area. Table 4.5 explores movement at police division level, and as can be seen there are still 80 per cent of matches with no significant movement.

Table 4.5: DNA matches Greater Manchester Police: divisional level

Non-adjacent division (any force)	20	(210)
Adjacent division (any force)	17	(176)
Within division	63	(669)

Note
1. Total n = 1154. 99 records were excluded from the analysis because the coding did not allow the identification of the relevant police division.

Overall the DNA database suggests that the vast majority of crime is a relatively localised phenomenon and that patterns of offender travel appear to conform to wider patterns of travel (that is, between urban and adjoining suburban areas and longer distance travel between urban and tourist areas).

5   Offender interviews

A group of offenders aged 16 to 43 years from Sheffield were interviewed. Half of the sample of offenders had been convicted of burglary offences, with the remaining half being convicted of TWOC, but as Table 5.1 shows, many had committed other offences too. Indeed, Over 50 per cent of 'burglars' had committed a TWOC and over 50 per cent of 'TWOCers' had committed a burglary. 'Burglars' were much more likely to have shoplifted or committed drug offences and 'TWOCers' were much more likely to have committed theft from a vehicle.

Table 5.1:   Self-reported offending of Sheffield interviewees

Offence	All as burglars		Interviewed as TWOCers		Interviewed	
	(%)	(n)	(%)	(n)	(%)	(n)
Burglary	82	(49)	-		56	(14)
TWOC	77	(46)	60	(21)		-
Shoplifting	47	(28)	57	(20)	32	(8)
Theft from Vehicle	35	(21)	26	(9)	48	(12)
Robbery	23	(14)	17	(6)	32	(8)
Violence	45	(27)	40	(14)	52	(13)
Other theft	58	(35)	69	(24)	44	(11)
Ram Raid	7	(4)	6	(2)	8	(2)
Sexual Offences	3	(2)	3	(1)	4	(1)
Damage/Arson	20	(12)	17	(6)	24	(6)
Drugs (excluding cannabis)	70	(42)	80	(28)	56	(14)

Note
1.   Percentages add up to over 100 because of multiple answers.

Overall the offending profile of the interviewees is consistent with other research findings that most offenders are generalists and opportunists rather than specialists. All admitted to carrying out more than one type of offence and one offender admitted nine different types of crime.

The structure of the interviews

The interviews all followed the same basic format with the interviewee being asked a series of set questions and then being invited to participate in an open-ended discussion about their pattern of offending and general lifestyle.

The structured interviews asked about pre-prison residence and whether it would be returned to. The offenders were then shown a map of the city and asked about their knowledge of 23 pre-identified neighbourhoods[19]. This was to ascertain whether the area was known to the offender, and if so, why; and whether the area was avoided, and if so, why this was the case. The offenders were then asked how they normally travelled around the city. The next questions were about areas outside Sheffield that they visited and why. They were then asked about their work/educational experience.

Only at this point were questions about offending introduced. The interviewees were asked detailed questions about their index offence[20], and further data was sought about up to three other offences.

Background details

With regard to pre-prison accommodation, 60 per cent lived with their parents or other relatives, 20 per cent in their own home or with a girlfriend and another 12 per cent lived in a local authority home. The average length of time at the pre-prison address was 5.5 years, with the shortest under one month and the longest 23 years. However, there was a basic divide between length of residence, with 43 per cent of the interviewees living at their most recent address for less than 12 months and 45 per cent for over 3 years. Of the offenders living with their parents or other relatives, primarily the younger ones, the average length of time at their current address was 9.5 years. Sixty percent said they would be returning to their pre-prison address on release. Half of the interviewees spent an average of seven nights a week at their home address and only 10 per cent spent less than two nights a week at home; there was no difference between burglars and TWOCers, and no difference between those living with their parents and the rest. Of those who said they would not be returning to their pre-prison address, almost three-quarters had not regarded it as a permanent address anyway.

---

19 The city was divided up into areas based upon our knowledge of the city and interviewees were shown these on a map. The interviewees appeared not to have any difficulty recognising the areas we had identified or using the map. Only one potential interviewee refused to participate in the research

20 The offence that led to their selection for interview.

Two-thirds of the interviewees had been unemployed at the time they committed their offence, with only 16 per cent working full- or part-time. Furthermore, three-quarters of the interviewees had no formal qualifications so were not in a strong position to enter the job market upon release. This lack of involvement in the labour market meant there was little point in analysing movement patterns in relation to place of work, even though some previous research has suggested that workplace is an important 'anchor point' around which offenders structure their movements (Brantingham and Brantingham, 1994).

The problem of poor educational attainment was compounded by the fact that during the course of the interviews it became apparent that well over half of the offenders were hard drug users (overwhelmingly heroin). This would appear to support Bennett's (1998) recent findings of the high incidence of drug use amongst those arrested. It is important to note that the use of hard drugs was extremely skewed: only 40 per cent of the TWOCers admitted to a hard drug problem whereas this figure rose to 69 per cent for the burglars. As will be seen, perhaps drug use is the main way of differentiating between the burglars and TWOCers. It certainly had an impact upon the reason for offending and the location of the offence.

Offenders' knowledge of the city

Almost half (45%) of the interviewees (excluding those offenders living in a local authority home) had lived in two or less of the 23 neighbourhoods pre-identified for the interviews. Moreover, 68 per cent had lived in six or less neighbourhoods; all were areas dominated by unpopular social housing.

When the interviewees were asked which of the areas they knew, the following findings emerged:

- on average each offender claimed to know 14 of the 23 areas; with the burglars claiming knowledge of just under 13 areas and the TWOCers claiming to know just over 15 areas. The areas known by the two groups were largely the same[21].

- the only area known by all the offenders was the city centre.

- another seven areas were known by over 66 per cent of interviewees, of these six are high offender/offence, unpopular social housing areas, and the other is a shopping and entertainment area in north Sheffield.

21 The correlation between burglars' knowledge of areas and the TWOCers was +0.7879 which is significant at the 0.1 per cent level.

- six of the areas were known by less than 50 per cent of the respondents. On the whole these are working class/lower middle class suburbs on the edge of the city without high offender rates.

Why some areas are known and others not can at least be partially explained by where the interviewees had lived. Of the least known areas none had been lived in by more than 13 per cent of the interviewees. However, the six well-known high offender/offence rate areas had been lived in by between 32 per cent and 48 per cent of the interviewees. On average each offender has lived in 4.4 neighbourhoods and the sample produced 264 lived in/area matches. Of these 139 (53%) were formed by the six highest offender rate neighbourhoods in the city. Each offender also said that they had friends in these areas at rates between 82 per cent and 96 per cent. Unsurprisingly these areas were also ones where the offenders had the strongest family links. These interview findings tended to confirm police recorded data on offender residence: the 10 per cent of census enumeration districts with the highest number of recorded offenders contained over 35 per cent of offender addresses.

On average each interviewee avoided 1.5 areas. The reasons for avoiding areas varied considerably. Of the three most avoided areas one is a high offender rate inner-city area, which is considered to be the centre of the city's drug trade, another is a high crime council estate and the third is a lower middle class/working class area on the north-western edge of the city (one of the least known parts of the city according to the interviewees). The main reasons given for avoiding an area were fear of a particular individual and being too well known by the local police. What did not emerge was any real sense that offenders were avoiding middle class areas because they believed they would not fit in or would stand out, even though the interviews probed for this reason on the basis that previous research has suggested that offenders will avoid such areas because they will feel 'ontologically insecure' (see, for example, Carter and Hill,1979). A much more prosaic reason for avoiding middle-class areas emerged – the offenders simply did not know them to any extent.

Travel around the city

Most of those interviewed (72%) said they had access to a car or motorbike; but the TWOCers had more access (92%) than the burglars (57%). This translated into the findings in Table 5.2 with regard to 'normal' modes of travel used to get round the city.

Whilst the TWOCers had the opportunity to be more legitimately mobile than the burglars did, they nevertheless were more likely to steal a car in order to be mobile. Furthermore, the TWOCers were significantly less likely to walk as a means of travel.

Table 5.2: *Modes of travel normally used to get around Sheffield*

Mode of travel	All		Burglars		TWOCers	
	(%)	(n)	(%)	(n)	(%)	(n)
Own Vehicle	60	(36)	49	(17)	76	(19)
Mate's Vehicle	85	(51)	77	(27)	96	(24)
Bus/Tram	83	(50)	86	(30)	80	(20)
Taxi	75	(45)	77	(27)	72	(18)
Walk	53	(32)	77	(27)	20	(5)
Bike	47	(28)	29	(10)	72	(18)
Stolen Car	72	(43)	51	(18)	100	(25)

Note
1. Percentages add up to over 100 because of multiple answers.

Travel to areas outside Sheffield

Each of the interviewees were given the opportunity to identify up to four places they visited outside the city on a regular basis. Just over a third (38%) replied that they had no regular visits outside the city. There was no particular age bias to this reply. The remaining 37 interviewees mentioned 68 places as set out in Table 5.3 and they are not dissimilar to the places that police recorded crime data shows Sheffielders offended in (see Table 3.5). Furthermore, 74 per cent of places are in the immediate vicinity of Sheffield and, if Skegness is included, 80 per cent of places have very close links with Sheffield.

Table 5.3: *Places regularly visited by Sheffield offenders and places travelled to primarily to offend*

Place	Visiting regularly		Visiting to offend	
	(%)	(n)	(%)	(n)
Rotherham	31	(21)	33	(11)
Chesterfield/North East Derbyshire	22	(15)	24	(8)
Doncaster	15	(10)	12	(4)
Barnsley	6	(4)	9	(3)
Skegness	7	(5)	12	(4)
Leeds	6	(4)	-	
Other	13	(9)	9	(3)
Total		68		33

The interview responses showed that offending was the single most important reason for visits outside the city, but this was outweighed collectively by other reasons. The places visited primarily in order to offend were very similar to those regularly visited for other reasons (see Table 5.3) and again are close to and closely connected with Sheffield.

Table 5.4:   Reasons for going to places outside Sheffield

Reason for visit	(%)	(n)
Relative/friends	39	(28)
Shopping	3	(2)
To offend	46	(33)
Work	4	(3)
Holidays	8	(6)
Total	72	

Offender travel-to-crime

The interview data provided the opportunity to analyse, in detail, the travel patterns of 90 burglaries and 72 TWOCs (7 burglaries and 3 TWOCs were lost because the offender could remember little of the offence, usually because of drugs). The spread of offending was wider than the spread of offender residence and only one of the 23 neighbourhoods (Meadowhall) did not have a burglary or TWOC. In other words, the concentration of offence locations is wider than the concentration of offender residences. Analysis of these offences in relation to the offenders' most recent address, areas previously lived in and areas known well (see Table 5.5), revealed that offences were most concentrated in the area of current residence, followed by areas previously lived in and finally areas known well.

Table 5.5:   Correlations with offence locations

Independent variables	Correlations
Areas lived in at some time	+0.6220 **
Areas known well	+0.3916 *
Areas currently lived in.	+0.7963 ***

Notes
1. *** significant at the 0.1 per cent level; ** significant at the 1 per cent level; significant at the 5 per cent level.
2. All the above correlations based upon Pearson Correlation Coefficient 1-tailed test.

As can be seen all are statistically significant, the most important being area of current residence which shows a very strong correlation. This confirms the earlier findings about the generally short distances travelled to offend. It also reinforces the importance of the earlier finding that offenders tended to live in, and move around, a relatively small number of residential areas of the city which had high, resident offender-driven offence rates.

Interviewees travel-to-crime

The interview data was also directly compared with the Sheffield recorded crime data. For each offence the offenders were asked where they had slept the night before the offence and why they were in the area of offence commission. Table 5.6 shows the average offender travel distances to offend, for burglary and TWOC, based on (a) police data using place of offence and recorded home address of the offender; (b) the interview data using place of offence and home address of the offender; and (c) interview data using place of offence and the address where the offender slept the night before the offence was committed.

Table 5.6: *Offender travel: police data and interview data*

	Burglary (miles)			TWOC (miles)		
	Recorded crime	Interview data		Recorded crime	Interview data	
	Police data travel (a)	Apparent travel (b)	Real travel (c)	Police data travel (a)	Apparent travel (b)	Real travel (c)
All offences	5.2	5.2	1.6	7.1	2.9	2.5
Within City offences	1.8	2.0	1.6	2.4	2.5	2.1
Out of City offences	31.4	38.5	1.0	30.8	6.5	6.5

Generally the short distances travelled to offend shown by police recorded crime statistics are an overestimate. For example, one of the interviewees committed two burglaries in Skegness, 90 miles from his home address in Sheffield. However, he was on holiday in Skegness and simply came across opportunities that were too tempting. The main point to note is the analysis based on police data is, if anything, likely to overestimate the distances travelled by offenders to offend.

There is some evidence that TWOCers are more likely to travel with the intention of offending than burglars (see Table 5.7) but the differences are not very great. Whilst offending is a significant reason for being in an area, overall it is less important than other non-criminal lifestyle reasons.

Table 5.7:   Reason for being in area of offence commission

Reason	All offences (%)	Burglary (%)	TWOC (%)
To offend	33	30	38
Near home	33	36	29
Chance	10	9	11
Visiting friends etc.	13	13	12
Leisure/shopping	7	7	7
Can't remember	4	5	2

There seems to be a greater search for an opportunity in the case of TWOC than burglary and this might be explained by the reason given for deciding to commit an offence, as shown in Table 5.8. The difference between reasons for being in an area (taking 'to offend' versus the rest) is significant at the 5 per cent level.

Table 5.8:   Reason for deciding to offend (index offences)

Reason	All offences (%)[22]	Burglary (%)	TWOC (%)
Easy Target/Good Opportunity	45	31	64
Needed Money	73	100	36
Bored	18	0	44
Drunk/Drugged Up	45	40	52
Influence of Mates	17	11	24
Fun	32	0	76
Other	17	11	24
Don't Know	0	0	0

Note
1. Percentages add up to over 100 because of multiple answers.

The main reported motivation for burglary is the need for money which was primarily for drugs. Car theft, on the other hand, is much more driven by the search for fun, with money a secondary issue even though most of the interviewees admitted they made money from car theft. The 'social' nature of TWOC can be illustrated by the joint nature of much TWOCing as opposed to burglary (see Table 5.9). Whilst over half of burglaries were carried out alone this drops to a fifth for TWOC and seems to confirm the different reasons for offending.

Table 5.9: Solo and joint offending

Number of Offenders	All offences		Burglary		TWOC	
	(%)	(n)	(%)	(n)	(%)	(n)
Solo	37	(61)	51	(46)	20	(15)
1 other	40	(66)	36	(32)	46	(34)
2-3 others	21	(33)	12	(11)	30	(22)
4 or more	3	(4)	1	(1)	4	(3)

One important aspect of drug-related offending that came across anecdotally in the interviews is that the burglars believe that they get caught as a result of being reckless because the need for drugs has become pressing. They offended very close to home and in an unplanned way and argued that this was why they were caught. However, this may be post-hoc rationalisation as almost as many burglars who travelled (n=9) as those who did not (n=11) were drug addicts[22]. Of the TWOCers, six non-travellers and four travellers were addicts.

Table 5.10: Target selection: TWOC (index offence)

Reason for selection	No.	(%)
Nearby and available	13	(52)
Easy to steal	22	(88)
Type of car I usually take	6	(24)
Good car (i.e. stylish, fast)	8	(32)
Looking for that type (make money)	5	(20)
Chance	12	(48)
Other	2	(8)

Note
1. Percentages add up to over 100 because of multiple answers.

22 Four of the five professionals were also drug users.

The financial imperatives for TWOCers seemed to be way down the list when compared with how easy the car was to steal, its availability and chance (Table 5.10). These answers might add weight to the findings of the Home Office's recent Car Crime Index which found that various older cars were the most likely to be stolen. Older cars generally have less sophisticated security systems than more modern cars, but they also are more likely to be owned by people living in the same residential areas as offenders are, thus contributing availability and chance.

Table 5.11: Target selection: burglary (index offence)

Reason for selection	(%)	(n)
Chance	63	(22)
Passing and looked easy (poor security)	31	(11)
Passing and looked easy (unoccupied)	26	(9)
Passing and looked easy (isolated/quiet)	26	(9)
Had noticed previously	20	(7)
Tipped off	17	(6)
Passing and looked wealthy	14	(5)
Revenge	6	(2)
Other	6	(2)
Burgled before	3	(1)

Note
1. Percentages add up to over 100 because of multiple answers.

Table 5.11 shows that the dominant reason for burglary target selection seems to be chance, either literally or in the sense that the offender just happened to be passing, whilst the proportion deliberately targeted was small.[23] One point that is worth making is the fact that repeat targeting appears uncommon and yet much recent research has suggested that offenders returning to the same target is a cause of repeat victimisation[24]. There was no evidence of significant repeat burglary targeting among those admitted by the interviewees.

23 The offenders themselves treated these categories as mutually exclusive.
24 Although this suggestion has been made and been supported by some empirical evidence the evidential base is still presently slim (see Pease, 1998 for a review of this literature).

The identification of travellers versus non-travellers

The research design was constructed so those offenders who appeared to travel and those who did not, holding age constant, could be compared (see Chapter 2). Travellers were defined as those offenders who for the index offence had travelled at least 2 miles. The travel patterns of the interviewees are shown in Table 5.12.

Table 5.12: Travel patterns of 'travellers' and 'non-travellers'.

	Index Offence: Apparent Travel	Index Offence: Real Travel	Other Burglary/ TWOC: Apparent Travel	Other Burglary/ TWOC: Real Travel
Travelling Burglars	3.6 miles	2.7 miles	12.8 miles	1.3 miles
Non Travelling Burglars	1.8 miles	0.4 miles	3.5 miles	0.6 miles
Travelling TWOCers	5.1 miles	3.8 miles	3.1 miles	2.5 miles
Non-Travelling TWOCers	0.2 miles	0.2 miles	1.9 miles	1.7 miles

The differences between travellers and non-travellers becomes much less apparent when offences other than the index offence for which they were selected are examined. This confirms the interview data in which there did not appear to be any discernible difference between the travellers and non-travellers. There was no difference between the two groups in terms of issues such as type of offences admitted to, mode of travel round the city, or knowledge of the city's areas. In other words, the data does not support the idea that some offenders are regular travellers and others not.

The group of professional offenders who were identified by South Yorkshire police produced the travel distances shown in Table 5.13.

Table 5.13: Travel of 'professional' offenders.

	Apparent Travel	Real Travel
Burglars	1.5 miles	1.4 miles
TWOCers	4.0 miles	3.4 miles

Given the relatively small sample of professionals it is difficult to say whether there are any differences from the main body of interviewees, although the interviews did not suggest any significant differences in terms of travel, target selection or reasons for offending[25].

Perhaps the main finding, with regard to travel, from the offender interviews is the broad confirmation it appears to give to the police and DNA data which suggests that patterns of travel can be broadly established by using police data. In fact as has been noted above, police data, if anything, overestimates travel.

Offender travel must also be seen in the context of anchor points such as the offender's home, or a friend's or girlfriend's home, or leisure location. However, even these anchor points are not simply related to non-criminal routines. For example, Figure 1 shows the pattern of burglaries committed by a single Sheffield offender relative to his home. As can be seen there are two clusters of burglaries: the larger cluster is around the offender's home but a secondary cluster is further to the south. In this case the secondary cluster is around the place where the offender regularly goes to buy drugs. The existence of a drug market in an area may increase crime rates as people offend on their way to buy drugs; it is relatively common for goods to be swapped for drugs. In the American context Rengert (1992) has argued that the location of drug markets are important anchor points for drug-dependent criminals who fund their purchases of drugs through property crime. Offending patterns may be largely driven by routine activities but offenders do not inhabit a world in which offending and non-offending routines are straightforwardly dichotomised. Offending, therefore, fits in with other routines as opportunities, needs or temptations present themselves and routines themselves can include both deviant and non-deviant behaviour.

---

25 The reason for the lack of difference may be that the professionals identified for us were drawn from the police list of the most prolific 25 burglars and 25 TWOCers in the city. There are, of course, other notions of 'professional' which the police could have applied.

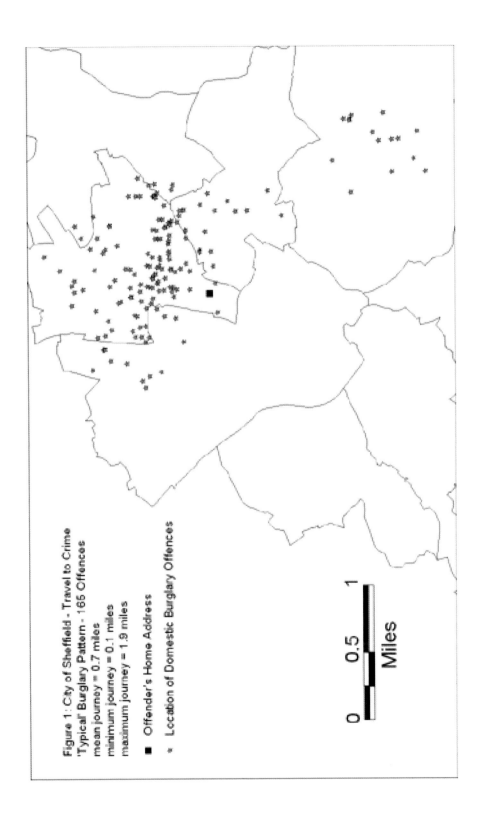

Figure 1: City of Sheffield - Travel to Crime
'Typical' Burglary Pattern - 165 Offences
mean journey = 0.7 miles
minimum journey = 0.1 miles
maximum journey = 1.9 miles

■ Offender's Home Address

* Location of Domestic Burglary Offences

0   0.5   1
Miles

On the basis of the evidence gathered a number of conclusions can be drawn about the offender movement patterns involved in high volume crimes.

Firstly, the vast majority of offender movements are relatively short: for Sheffield-based offenders (regardless of offence location) police recorded crime data shows that over a third of crime trips are less than one mile; over 50 per cent consist of less than two miles and only 11 per cent involve travel greater than 10 miles. There has, however, been some small increase in travel-to-crime distances over the last thirty years. Whilst data is not available on Sheffield commuting-to-work, it is likely that it would involve greater distances than journeys to crime and has probably increased more over the last thirty years. In general it is probably the case that persistent offenders travel less (whether to offend or for other reasons) than the rest of the population. Recent Department of Environment, Transport and the Regions research (DETR, 1999) supports our argument in that it shows the better-off travel much more than the poor. In 1995/97 the average distance travelled per annum for the top 20 per cent of the population (in terms of income) was about 11,000 miles but for the bottom 20 per cent it was only around 3,500 miles. Journeys for work or leisure average around 8 miles, whereas journeys for education or shopping average only 2.75 and 3.75 miles respectively. The interviewees were little involved in journeys to work and their leisure travel was largely short-range. Furthermore, even for shopping and education it is likely to be the wealthier groups in society who are more likely to travel to a 'better school' or an out of town shopping facility. This finding is not surprising given the short travel-to-crime journeys found in earlier research in more mobile North American cities (see Chapter 1). The Sheffield findings are confirmed by those from the city of York, where the vast majority of burglary and TWOC offenders live locally and, if anything, travel even shorter distances to offend, and by the analysis of the national DNA data.

Secondly, the research indicates that much travel associated with crime is not primarily driven by plans to offend. The offenders interviewed did not travel to the offence location in order to offend in the majority of instances (70% for burglary and 62% for TWOC). Offending appeared to be much more dependent upon opportunities presenting themselves during normal routines, rather than as a result of instrumental, long-range search patterns. This is further supported by the fact that the strongest correlation found was between offence location and the current residence of the offender.

Thirdly, when offenders do travel to offend it is overwhelmingly local in nature. Indeed, of all trips over three miles by Sheffield-based offenders, 55 per cent were wholly within the city. Even when offending crossed local authority borders most offence locations of Sheffield-based offenders had strong connections with the city. Forty percent of Sheffield offender movements out of the city ended up in either Rotherham or North East Derbyshire, both places with strong work, leisure and family ties to the city and lengthy and often indistinguishable boundaries. This pattern was confirmed by the interviews with the offender sample, where the places they visited for non-crime reasons were by and large the same as those recorded when Sheffielders offended outside the city. If anything the pattern of offender movements into Sheffield was even more restricted with almost half (46%) of offender movements originating in the adjoining town of Rotherham. The findings from the city of York confirm these findings with 94 per cent of burglary and 84 per cent of TWOC offender movements originating within the city.

Fourthly, even when longer-range travel was involved in offending elsewhere this was mainly in places which had strong traditional connections with Sheffield (such as Skegness) or were obvious leisure trips (such as southern seaside resorts or London).

Overall there was little evidence that offender's travelling to offend was significantly increasing compared with the past or that new travel opportunities were changing traditional travel patterns used by offenders. Indeed, an overwhelming impression was just how traditional the travel behaviour of the offenders was. Theories of late modernity, or post-modernism, have argued that various global forces are undermining traditional social structures and culture and this will ultimately affect crime patterns (see for example Bottoms and Wiles, 1995). As far as the travel patterns of the offenders were concerned there is little sign of such changes. Given what is known generally about persistent and repeat offenders, then these limited travel patterns are not surprising. Long-range travel, like much other human activity, requires knowledge, confidence, skills and resources. However, the risk factors associated with offending are either the lack of such skills or are closely correlated with them. Offenders generally do not travel long distances because they are drawn from those groups in the population who lack the personal and material resources to learn to travel and sustain such travel thereafter.

Whilst these findings were confirmed by interview data, the general patterns could all be identified from police recorded crime data. This is important because police recorded crime data is already available for the whole country and does not require the additional cost and difficulty of interviewing offenders. However, police data tends to overestimate travel. This is because using home address and offence location to measure travel distance produces noticeably larger figures than using offence location and where the offender spent the night prior to the offence. Again this finding illustrates that offender travel is not primarily about offending, but is mainly related to routines such as staying at a friend's or girlfriend's house, thus the location of the offence is not determined by instrumental search patterns except over short ranges. Earlier research has discussed the extent to which patterned routine activities produce 'anchor points' (such as home, place of work or place of leisure) around which offending is carried out. In this study, persistent offenders had little contact with a world of regularised work and lacked the resources for stable leisure pursuits. The one clear anchor point which emerged, therefore, was their home. However, since their lives were largely irregular, spontaneous and unstructured, then alternative and temporary 'anchor points', such as a girlfriend's home, came and went although always within a limited number of the city's neighbourhoods.

The behaviour of the known offenders who committed high volume crimes is dominated by opportunistic offending during routine and limited travel patterns. However, this is not to deny that there may be 'professional travelling criminals'; just to deny they are responsible for much high volume crime. An attempt was made to examine this possibility in the research by interviewing a small group of offenders who had been identified by the police as 'professionals'. However, the sense of 'professional' used by the police was 'persistent' and their travel patterns were not distinct. Future research could well examine other senses of 'professional' perhaps by investigating particular types of crime. For example, country house rather than council estate burglaries might be one starting point or the theft of valuable cars where joyriding does not seem to be the prime motive may be another.

Given the foregoing and other research we have conducted into crime patterns, particularly in Sheffield, we feel confident in asserting that, generally, high volume crime is a highly localised phenomenon, especially for offences such as domestic burglary and criminal damage. Residential areas with high offence and victimisation rates are generally found on poorer social housing estates, and some mixed inner-city areas. We can suggest this highly localised pattern holds for a number of reasons:

1. Even poor areas contain plenty of suitable targets such as videos, televisions and cars. Recent Home Office research into car crime, for example, appears to support the notion of localised victimisation as it shows the highest rates of theft for older cars of the type that predominate in poorer areas of Britain (Houghton, 1992).

2. Offenders tend to live in these areas and also, on the whole, tend to offend close to home rather than conduct long-range instrumental searches across a city. The Sheffield interviewees generally lived in a restricted number of the poorer social housing areas of the city – what we have termed 'impacted crime areas'.

3. The other areas the offenders knew (other than the city centre) were similar in character to the one they currently lived in and usually they had either lived in them previously or had friends or family in the area. The result is that even if offending is carried out away from home it tends to be in areas where offenders have contacts, not unknown middle-class parts of the city.

These factors mean that a city's broad crime patterns tend to be stable and predictable in the short-term. High offence and victim rate areas are the parts of a city where offenders tend to live and are generally the parts of a city which are considered least desirable in terms of residential location. Such patterns will be self-reinforcing through mechanisms such as the housing market and allocation systems unless other macro policy or market factors disrupt them.

The result, in the case of Sheffield, has been that even in the long term some aspects of crime patterns appear to be fairly stable. Some of the areas with 'impacted' crime patterns in the 1960s (see Baldwin and Bottoms, 1976) appear to be the same today, and the broad geographical crime pattern of Sheffield is little changed over thirty years. However, it is not the case that all patterns of crime remain static, and important changes in the fabric of the city have had an impact upon crime patterns. In Sheffield these have included: the redevelopment of once private rental areas of the city; the growth of a new private rental sector catering for the growing number of students; the demolition of unpopular areas of public housing which has changed the relative unpopularity of the remaining areas; the development of out of town retailing (such as Meadowhall shopping mall), which has seen the city centre's share of all offences decline from 25 per cent in 1966 to 10 per cent in 1995; and changes in the demographic profiles of neighbourhoods which have shifted their community crime careers. It is likely that a similar mixture of stability and change would be found in other British cities.

Crime management

Offender travel patterns and how these change over time are one way of examining the crime patterns of cities and thinking about appropriate strategic crime management responses. However, the GIS techniques used for this study can equally be used to examine how far victims travel before they are victimised. From what has already been reported there are obvious relationships between the relative offence and offender rates of residential neighbourhoods and the travel patterns of offenders who offend in an area. If we simply categorise the residential neighbourhoods of a city in terms of whether they have a high/medium/low offence rate and offender rate[26] then in theory we might expect to find the possibilities shown in Table 33, in which there are nine possible crime type areas. In practice some of these are very unlikely to exist. For example, a high offender/low offence rate residential area is unlikely.

Table 6.1:   *Crime type areas based on simple trichotomy*

Offender rate	Offence rate		
	high	medium	low
high	*high/high*	*high/medium*	*high/low*
medium	*medium/high*	*medium/medium*	*medium/low*
low	*low/high*	*low/medium*	*low/low*

For each of these crime type areas we can then examine the travel patterns of those known offenders who committed their offence in the area and the travel patterns of area residents when they are victimised. Doing this will produce a 'crime travel footprint' to show how far and in what direction, on average, offenders travel to offend in the area and victims, who live in the area, travel before they are victimised[27]. In practice, for residential areas in Sheffield, we have only found four dominant crime travel footprints, of which three are the most common. Areas with high offence and offender rates; areas with low offence and offender rates; and areas with medium offence and offender rates are common. Very much less common are residential areas with high offence rates but low offender rates. The crime travel footprints for examples of each of these crime type areas are set out in Figures, 2, 3, 4 and 5.

Figure 2 shows the crime travel footprint for a low offence/low offender rate neighbourhood. The neighbourhood itself is made up of the census enumeration districts shaded on the map. Circle 1 shows the average distance and direction which victims who lived in the neighbourhood travelled before they were victimised, and circle 2 shows the average distance and direction in which the known offenders travelled who committed offences in the neighbourhood. What this travel crime footprint shows is that those who commit offences in the neighbourhood come predominately from outside, from a direction in which higher offender rate areas of the city are found and travel some distance to offend.

---

26 This is most easily done at enumeration district level (because that provides the population denominators to calculate rates) and by defining high/medium/low in terms of the trichotomy of the distribution of offence and offender rates for the city as a whole.

27 In Figures 2-5 the mean location refers to the mean centre of a series of spatial locations. It is calculated by averaging the x and y coordinates of a series of points as described in McGrew and Munroe (1993).

This reflects the fact that the area has a low offender rate. However, those who live in the neighbourhood also have to travel before their victimisation risk is heightened. This is largely because auto crime risks increase as the cars of those who live in the neighbourhood are parked elsewhere in the city nearer to high offender areas. Such a travel-to-crime footprint can be used to think about what kind of crime management would be appropriate. For example, since offenders are coming from outside the area then methods for monitoring the actions of outsiders (such as Neighbourhood Watch) might be useful. At the same time resident's cars are more vulnerable when they leave their neighbourhood and mapping where they park could be used to target protective strategies.

Figure 3 shows the travel-to-crime footprint of a high offence/high offender rate neighbourhood. As can be seen the two travel circles are this time tightly drawn around the area, which indicates that most offences in the area are committed by offenders who live nearby and that those who live in the area are most likely to be victimised in their own neighbourhood. This crime travel footprint is that classically associated with an impacted high crime area. Crime management strategies for such an area need to be different than those for the neighbourhood shown in Figure 1. For example, since local offenders are largely driving the victimisation rate, then any strategy is going to have to do something about the area's offender rate. At the same time we know that even in such impacted high crime areas not all households are victimised and so a mapping of concentrated and repeat victimisation ought to be the basis for protective responses.

The same data is shown in figures 4, and 5, but for a medium offence/offender rate area and a high offence/low offender rate area respectively. The general point is that the different area crime travel footprints can be used as the basis for developing different neighbourhood crime management strategies designed to respond to the particular relationship between offender travel and victim travel-to-crime. Such footprints are straightforward to produce with geocoded crime data and could usefully be incorporated into area crime audits to help determine the appropriate crime management strategies for each neighbourhood of a city.

We referred in the Introduction to the future importance of GIS for the use of police-held data. A key lesson from previous attempts to reduce crime or offending is that success depends crucially on a careful identification of the crime problem that is to be tackled. Crime per se cannot be prevented; the focus should be on particular offences or offending in particular places and times. Geographical identification of crime problems is one necessary dimension and can be the key to layering police-held data onto other data sets (such as small area census data to produce rates of offending or offences) and to the partnership crime audits required by the Crime and Disorder Act 1998. Furthermore, any police commander will want a careful analysis of their area's crime problem as the basis for a policing plan. However, as the analysis has illustrated, the boundaries of police forces or divisions can be arbitrary and unless analysis can escape them then a proper understanding of crime problems can be impossible. The ability of future police data systems to both geo-analyse data, and to link different data systems, will be crucial to overcoming such problems.

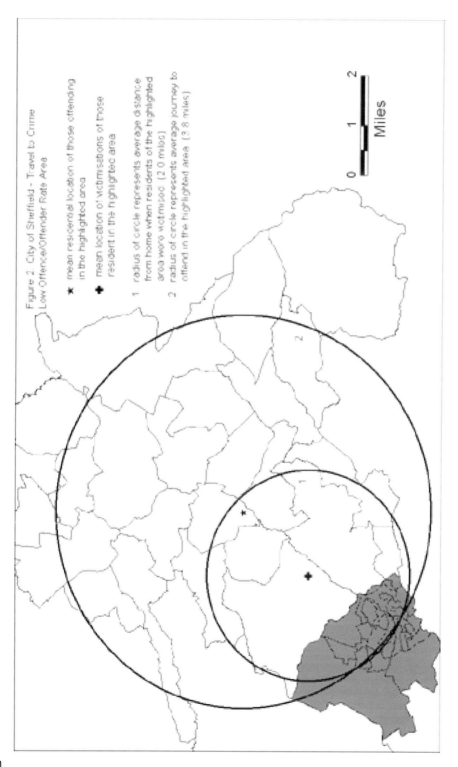

Figure 2 City of Sheffield – Travel to Crime
Low Offence/Offender Rate Area

✳ mean residential location of those offending in the highlighted area

✚ mean location of victimisations of those resident in the highlighted area

1 radius of circle represents average distance from home when residents of the highlighted area were victimised (2.0 miles)

2 radius of circle represents average journey to offend in the highlighted area (3.8 miles)

Miles
0   1   2

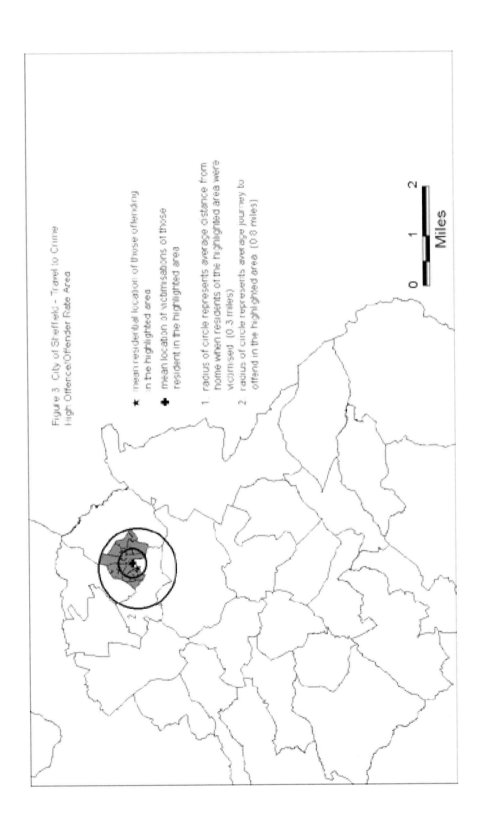

Figure 3 City of Sheffield - Travel to Crime
High Offence/Offender Rate Area

★ mean residential location of those offending
   in the highlighted area

✛ mean location of victimisations of those
   resident in the highlighted area

1 radius of circle represents average distance from
   home when residents of the highlighted area were
   victimised (0.3 miles)

2 radius of circle represents average journey to
   offend in the highlighted area (0.8 miles)

0   1   2
Miles

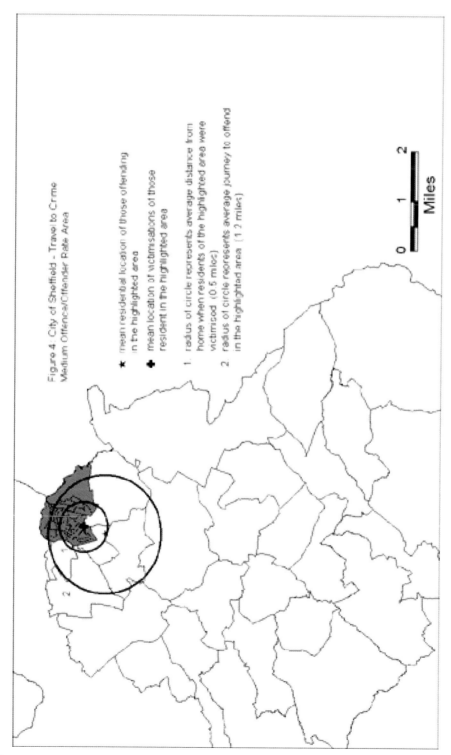

Figure 4. City of Sheffield – Travel to Crime
Medium Offence/Offender Rate Area

★   mean residential location of those offending
    in the highlighted area

✚   mean location of victimisations of those
    resident in the highlighted area

1. radius of circle represents average distance from
    home when residents of the highlighted area were
    victimised (0.5 miles)

2. radius of circle represents average journey to offend
    in the highlighted area (1.2 miles)

0   1   2
Miles

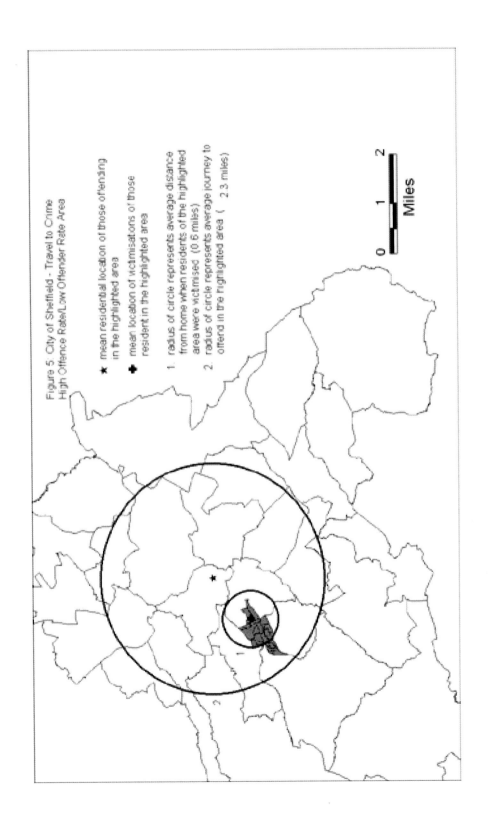

Figure 5: City of Sheffield - Travel to Crime
High Offence Rate/Low Offender Rate Area

★ mean residential location of those offending in the highlighted area

✚ mean location of victimisations of those resident in the highlighted area

1. radius of circle represents average distance from home when residents of the highlighted area were victimised (0.6 miles)

2. radius of circle represents average journey to offend in the highlighted area (2.3 miles)

0   1   2
Miles

References

BALDWIN, J. and BOTTOMS, A. (1976) *The Urban Criminal: A Study in Sheffield;* London: Tavistock.

BENNETT, T. (1998) *Drugs and Crime: the results of research on drug testing and interviewing of arrestees;* Home Office Research Study 183. London: Home Office.

BOTTOMS, A.E. and WILES, P. (1999) 'Environmental Criminology', in M. Maguire, R. Morgan and R. Reiner (eds.) *The Oxford Handbook of Criminology;* 2nd Edition, Oxford: Clarendon.

BOTTOMS, A.E. and WILES, P. (1995) 'Crime and Insecurity in the City' in C. Fijnaut et al (eds.) *Changes in Society, Crime and Criminal Justice in Europe* 2 vols.; The Hague: Kluwer.

BRANTINGHAM, P. and BRANTINGHAM, P. (1994) 'Burglar Mobility and Crime Prevention', in R. Clarke and T. Hope (eds.) *Coping with Burglary.* Boston; MA: Kluwer Nijhoff.

CARTER, R.L. and HILL, K.Q. (1979) *The Criminal's Image of the City;* New York: Pergamon.

DAVIDSON, R.N. (1984) 'Burglary in the Community: Patterns of Localisation in Offender-Victim Relations', in R. Clarke and T. Hope (eds.) *Coping with Burglary;* Boston, MA: Kluwer Nijhoff.

DETR (1999) *A Better Quality of Life: A Strategy for Sustainable Development for the United Kingdom* Cm 4345]

GABOR, T. and GOTTHEIL, E. (1984) 'Offender Characteristics and Spatial Mobility: An Empirical Study and Some Policy Implications'; *Canadian Journal of Criminology* 26: 267-281.

HOUGHTON, G. (1992) 'Car Crime in England and Wales: The Home Office Car Theft Index'; *Crime Prevention Unit Paper 33;* London: Home Office.

McGREW, J.C. and MONROE, C.B. (1993) *An Introduction to Statistical Problem Solving in Geography;* Dubuque, Iowa: Wm Brown.

PHILLIPS, P.D. (1980) 'Characteristics and Typology of the Journey to Crime', in D.E. Georges-Abeyie and K.D. Harries (eds.) *Crime: A Spatial Perspective;* New York: Columbia University Press.

PORTER, M. (1996) 'Tackling Cross Border Crime' PRG *Crime Detection and Prevention Series Paper 79;* London: Home Office Police Department.

PYLE, G. (1974) 'The Spatial Dynamics of Crime' *Department of Geography Research Paper 159;* Chicago: University of Chicago Press.

RAND, A. (1986) ' Mobility Triangles'. In Figlio et al (eds.) *Metropolitan Crime Patterns;* Monsey, NY: Criminal Justice Press.

REISS, A.J. and FARRINGTON, D.P. (1991) 'Advancing Knowledge about Co-offending: Results from a Prospective Longitudinal Survey of London Males' *Journal of Criminal Law & Criminology,* 82(2): 360-395

RENGERT, G. and WASILCHICK, J. (1985) *Suburban Burglary;* Springfield, Ill: Charles Thomas.

REPPETTO, T.A. (1974) *Residential Crime;* Cambridge MA: Ballinger.

RHODES, W.M. and CONLY, C.C. (1981) 'Crime and Mobility', in P.J. Brantingham and P.L. Brantingham (eds.) *Environmental Criminology;* Beverly Hills: Sage.

ROSSMO, D.K. (1995) 'Place, Space and Police Investigations', in J. Eck and D. Weisburd (eds.) *Crime and Place;* Monsey, NY: Criminal Justice Press.

STOCKDALE, J.E. and GRESHAM, P.J. (1998) *Tackling Street Robbery: A Comparative Evaluation of Operation Eagle Eye* Crime Detection and Prevention Series, Paper 87. London: Home Office.

WHITE, R.C. (1932) 'The Relations of Felonies to Environmental Factors in Indianapolis' *Social Forces* 10: 498-509.

Notes

RDS Publications

Requests for Publications

Copies of our publications and a list of those currently available may be obtained from:

> Home Office
> Research, Development and Statistics Directorate
> Communications Development Unit
> Room 201, Home Office
> 50 Queen Anne's Gate
> London SW1H 9AT
> Telephone: 020 7273 2084 (answerphone outside of office hours)
> Facsimile: 020 7222 0211
> E-mail: publications.rds@homeoffice.gsi.gov.uk

alternatively

why not visit the RDS web-site at
> Internet: http://www.homeoffice.gov.uk/rds/index.htm

where many of our publications are availabe to be read on screen or downloaded for printing.